BITCOIN

Bitcoin and Cryptocurrency Basics, Investing in Bitcoin, Using Bitcoin in Business and How to Get Bitcoin Now: Written in Simple Language with a Quick Start Plan

© Copyright 2017 By Lee Sebastian
All rights reserved.

Published By:

Positive Impact Books
7579 E. Main Street
Suite 500
Scottsdale, AZ 85251
https://PositiveImpactBooks.com

"Check Out Our Other Cryptocurrency Titles and FREE Book Promotions at Our Website"

Disclaimer

This Book, *Bitcoin: Bitcoin and Cryptocurrency Basics, Investing in Bitcoin, Bitcoin in Businesses, and How to Get Bitcoin Now: Designed in Simple Language with a Quick Start Plan-* is reproduced below with the goal of providing information that is as accurate and reliable as possible. Regardless, purchasing this Book can be seen as consent to the fact that both the publisher and the author of this book are in no way experts on the topics discussed within and that any recommendations or suggestions that are made herein are for entertainment purposes only. Professionals should be consulted as needed prior to undertaking any of the action endorsed herein.

This declaration is deemed fair and valid by both the American Bar Association and the Committee of Publishers Association and is legally binding throughout the United States.

Furthermore, the transmission, duplication or reproduction of any of the following work including specific information will be considered an illegal act irrespective of if it is done electronically or in print. This extends to creating a secondary or tertiary copy of the work or a recorded copy and is only allowed with the express written consent of the Publisher. All additional right reserved.

The information in the following pages is broadly considered to be a truthful and accurate account of facts, and as such any inattention, use or misuse of the information in question by the reader will render any resulting actions solely under their purview. There are no scenarios in which the publisher or the original author of this work can be in any fashion deemed liable for any hardship or damages that may befall them after undertaking information described herein.

Additionally, the information in the following pages is intended only for informational purposes and should thus be thought of as universal. As befitting its nature, it is presented without assurance regarding its prolonged validity or interim quality. Trademarks that are mentioned are done without written consent and can in no way be considered an endorsement from the trademark holder.

Table of Contents

Introduction 1

Chapter 1: What is Bitcoin and Cryptocurrency? 3

Chapter 2: How Does Blockchain Work? 9

Chapter 3: How Do You Buy Bitcoins? 13

Chapter 4: How Do You Use Bitcoin? 19

Chapter 5: How Do You Use Bitcoin in Business? 21

Chapter 6: How Do You Invest in Bitcoin? 25

Chapter 7: How Secure Is Bitcoin? 33

Chapter 8: How Do You Remain Anonymous with Bitcoin? 37

Chapter 9: Why is Bitcoin So Popular? 43

Chapter 10: What Are the Consequences of Government Money? 49

Chapter 11: How to Start Using Bitcoin: (Interactive Links Included!) 51

Conclusion 53

INTRODUCTION

The world is ever changing with new technology, and people are constantly looking for new ways to improve their current lives. Although our technology system might not look much like what was envisioned in Disney's movie *Wall-E* or the futuristic drama *Back to the Future*, it has evolved in ways to where we now do almost everything online. We talk online, we shop online, and we practically live online. Because of this, we often manage our finances online, too. This allows us to innovate new methods to manage money online and take it into our own control with an better method. One new method has led an anonymous innovator named Satoshi to create a whole new anonymous system of currency online – a system known as Bitcoin.

Bitcoin might sound sketchy at first, and you may be concerned about how secure it is. But what if I told you that the system is completely free from the government's hands, and you finally get a currency with other people, backing up how much money you have? Rather than trusting that the government has enough funding to back up everyone's money (which they might not), you get a community of trusted people to watch your back in every financial matter. In addition, it is easy for you to use Bitcoin while transferring it to all currencies of the world. There are low processing fees and everything you do is completely anonymous and all up to you. That is right – the world of Bitcoin is nothing short of marvelous, and by buying this book today, you are taking the proactive step to understanding what may soon be the largest currency in the world! There are already more than ten million people who use Bitcoin, and buying this book will help you become part of the community!

From beginning to end, this book will explain the history of Bitcoin and the amazing founders behind it. This book will explain how you can buy, sell, and trade Bitcoins and use them for business. You will learn more than you have ever imagined about this currency. You will also learn about the benefits of Bitcoin.

Because of the rising popularity of Bitcoin, there are many books out there about this currency, its history, and how to use it. We are glad that you picked our book. It means a lot to us, and we promise that we will not disappoint. You will be happy that you chose ours out of all the precious books out there. Be sure to tell us if you have any suggestions, but for now, open away and learn as much as you can!

CHAPTER 1

WHAT IS BITCOIN AND CRYPTOCURRENCY?

Welcome to *Bitcoin: Bitcoin and Cryptocurrency Basics, Investing in Bitcoin, Bitcoin in Businesses, and How to Get Bitcoin Now: Designed in Simple Language with a Quick Start Plan!* We are going to discuss the concept of digital money. What comes to your mind when you hear the words "digital money"? Do you imagine money in debit cards that you can use to spend on Amazon Prime? Do you imagine eBay sellers and PayPal accounts and things similar to that? Well, Bitcoin and other types of cryptocurrency will take you to a whole new world that you would never have imagined.

To understand Bitcoins, we must first understand cryptocurrency. What exactly is cryptocurrency, you might ask? Well, if you think about it, currency is basically just a system of money that people use. And how exactly would we know how much money people have? All money requires data entries or entered information in a computer system that tells us how much we have spent and saved from our everyday lives. With the Internet and all this new technology coming out constantly, cryptocurrencies are now possible. Money has now moved online, and there are completely new systems of money that thrive on the world wide web. Cryptocurrency is digital money that requires a code to get into it – making it secure and mostly anonymous. The computers convert your information about money transactions, sales, and balances into computer codes that are nearly impossible to crack or break, making it harder to hack and easier to track your money if something somehow goes awry. This is what makes cryptocurrencies safe – even though everything is on the Internet!

How does this currency differ from the one we have now? Well, government money, such as the dollar bill, operates on a gold standard. This means that you can trade your cash for gold, according to the United States government (though you will probably never know if they have enough gold to supply everyone). With Bitcoin, you know that it is a completely transparent currency. People who uses the currency who volunteer to be a "miner," or someone who checks on other Bitcoin users, keep a record of every transaction that each person makes, making everyone as honest as can be.

This new currency has been growing since the late 2000s, and many people wonder about the genius behind this whole concept. Who thought about this idea? Well, it is none other than the anonymous guy known by the pseudonym *Satoshi Nakamoto*. He most likely remained anonymous just to protect his own identity and to promote the product in a light to where people would not harass him for creating an unsafe currency. People are now saying that Satoshi Nakamoto could be three people who just happened to file a patent a couple of months before the official release of Bitcoin. Their names were Neal Kin, Vladimir Oksman, and Charles Bry, but all of them deny having anything to do with Bitcoin or the Satoshi pseudonym.

We do not even know if the creator was from Japan or not. Even though they went by the name Satoshi (that is a name that means "wise") and Nakamoto (means a "foundation"), These terms describe Bitcoin to its core, so it is really hard to assume who the creator actually was. We do not know what he is really up to right now, except that he claimed he was on to bigger and better things. According to reports, though, the creator is one billion dollars richer because of Bitcoin!

The creators of Bitcoin were most excited to have their source of money "decentralized." This means that we control the system, not one person in power. It is equivalent to a government run by the people. That means that you do not need a middle man to manage the money. Instead, Bitcoins are managed by everyone who uses it – this is a system known as peer to peer by fellow Bitcoin users. Sooner than expected, Satoshi saw his plan grow in popularity! If you want to hear more about Satoshi's idea, click on this link here: SATOSHI'S GRAND SCHEME (www.bitcoin.org/bitcoin.pdf)

This abstract outlines everything that the anonymous man had planed for it. One by one, Satoshi decided that our financial system had too many flaws and mistakes in it. Not only do you have to go through a central authority, but you had to fully trust that they had all the valuables that they said they had. A good example of when our current money system did not work is the financial crisis of 2008. All around the world, people were experiencing losses because banks kept handing out loans with virtually no interest and devaluing the currency of each country to stay competitive in the world. With the banks printing out that much extra money, the government had to compensate, causing the money value to go down. You see, though, with Bitcoin, this does not happen. Bitcoin does not allow one person in the middle to make all the decisions, but rather everyone.

So how does this thing work, in simple terms? The price of Bitcoins is dependent on what we call "supply and demand" in economics. This means that the price of Bitcoin will go up as long as people trust it and buy it. Right now, twenty-one million Bitcoins are flowing around in the market until the year 2040. As demands go up, the price of Bitcoin may go up, so it is a good investment.

Like any currency system, there is a catch to Bitcoin. You need to believe in the system for it to work. We know that many people are not comfortable with change and want to stick to the stuff they know, but times are changing and so is our financial system. If you think about it, people used to use postal mail a lot more because texting wasn't invented yet. As we know now, texting is easier. Analogously, Bitcoin is as easy as that. With so many people keeping track of the flow of Bitcoins, it is not unsafe! Like anything else, it leaps faith. Nothing is guaranteed to be safe, but with the amount of people verifying the number of Bitcoins every person has, it is hard for it to be stolen from you. This is a system of faith.

As long as people have faith in the currency, it will continue to thrive.

We will now teach you how the basic heart of Bitcoin works, which is called the blockchain system.

CHAPTER 2

HOW DOES BLOCKCHAIN WORK?

Now that you know what Bitcoin is and a little bit about how it works, we are going to tell you a little bit about the heart of Bitcoin, or Blockchain. This is the reason why we can trust strangers to keep track of how many Bitcoins that we have. Blockchain is defined as a financial ledger that stores a history of financial transactions. For a simple video that explains the Blockchain, click this: Blockchain Explained. It is a system that uses your greedy nature to secure that Bitcoins are kept honest and safe. Because we do not want our Bitcoins devaluing, we will be honest about how much everyone else has. This financial ledger stores all transactions since its debut in 2009. This system is transparent, which means that everyone sees it. At the same time, however, it does not use names but rather a code to refer to people. Your transactions are still kept completely anonymous, which is what most people love! Many of you might be wondering what this public blockchain looks like. Here is a link to the biggest transparent public blockchain that stores all of Bitcoin's transactions. Take a look here at BLOCKCHAIN. (www.blockchain.info)

You might ask, why are we naming this system "blockchain?" Well, it has to do with how it works. Each "block" has multiple transactions stored in it. Every block after that has a "hash," a random arrangement of random numbers. When you spend Bitcoins, you have half of a key and the people checking you have another half of the key. This ensures that you cannot make a transaction until someone else verifies how many Bitcoins you have and makes sure that you have not spent the same Bitcoins somewhere else before because it would be located somewhere in the ledger. The blockchain helps to keep everyone honest, and it can send just about everything through a system that everyone can trust.

Here is an example of how Blockchain would work in a transaction:

- Ann wants to send a hundred Bitcoins to Megan.

- Bitcoins are spent, so Bitcoin and the blockchain would keep track of the money transfer in a "block."

- Everyone who is helping Bitcoin check for fraud (also called miners, which I will talk about in the next paragraph) sees the block in a giant networking community.

- The miners make sure that Ann is not trying to rip off everyone else in the Bitcoin community. They make sure that she has not spent the coins yet, and that she does indeed

- have the hundred Bitcoins that she is transferring to Megan.

- The hundred-Bitcoin transfer is approved by the community!

- We can now see the transaction block in the whole history of Bitcoin used or the public open ledger.

- Now, Megan has the money from Ann and can spend it on whatever she wants!

Now, who are all these people who are checking these transactions? If you are anything like us, you might be thinking... nobody has time for that! However, these people get paid in Bitcoins if they do their job correctly, which means that there is an incentive for them to do their job correctly! These people are called "nodes," and they are the computers for Bitcoin. That means that they also need decent math skills, but really, it is so basic that nearly anyone can run a computer for Bitcoin. When a transaction comes in, these computers get to work and make sure that the transaction is legit. Other computers confirm their work, and the first person who solves it gets the Bitcoins. A little friendly competition for money has helped to keep these computers honest and efficient. Once they are sure about their transaction, it is saved on the Blockchain for everyone to see in the future.

Only you have the private key to your block or the private code. This makes sure that blocks in the Blockchain cannot be edited, so someone cannot try to scam you. They cannot say that you spent a thousand dollars when you only spent a hundred.

For you to spend Bitcoins, it is easier if you create an online currency wallet. There are many programs out there that allow you to create a wallet. A wallet allows you to store your Bitcoins in it and trade them with other people for stuff. You can choose to get your wallet here today! (www.bitcoin.org/en/choose-your-wallet)

A wallet is defined by a key system – the one we were talking about earlier. When you trade bitcoins on your wallet, you can share your "public key" with the other person, but you still keep the private key or code to yourself. If both of your keys match by the end of the transaction, the transaction is complete! You need to make sure that you have your private key to send anything to anyone.

We are not going to go into the technical details about this, but feel free to search around the blockchain ledger. You are completely safe when everyone can secure your transactions.

CHAPTER 3

HOW DO YOU BUY BITCOINS?

Many of you might be wondering about this since you started reading this book. You might think that this sounds cool, but you might not know how to get your hands on Bitcoins at all. Bitcoins might seem hard to come by, but the reality is, they are one of the easiest things to obtain. You would need to go online to a "Bitcoin exchange." Bitcoin exchanges are usually websites that allow you to purchase coins. Anybody can sign up for an account and buy Bitcoins if they so desire. You need to have a few things before you can buy Bitcoins.

- A working laptop that allows you to get on the Internet is required.

- You need an email that you can register with a Bitcoin exchange website.

- You need to activate your account in your email so that you can start buying Bitcoins today!

Most people use the app or the website Coinbase, which is the most popular network for people to buy and sell Bitcoins. https://www.coinbase.com/

We recommend you use Coinbase to buy and sell Bitcoins instead of another website because it is the one most trusted and verified as of date.

Here is what the app can do once you get it from the Apple Store or Google Play. First, it shows you the value of Bitcoins, then it tells you to either login or signup. You can enter in your personal information to sign up. They will ask for your name, email address, and a password. Once you sign up, select your state, enter your address, and put in your phone number so that Bitcoin knows where you are and can register you as a new user. Since this is all online, you will need either a bank account number or a credit card that allows you to connect to the Internet. This is how you will trade your country's currency for Bitcoins.

The app itself is very simple. You simply select the currency you want once you are inside the app and logged in, and that would be Bitcoin. You would enter your payment method, which would be either your credit or debit card or maybe even your bank account. You enter in the amount of Bitcoins you want, and you press "Buy Bitcoin Instantly." When you confirm your transaction, you now have a bunch of Bitcoins to buy and sell!

We know by now that Bitcoin is safe, but you still need to understand that it is similar to a stock, and its value can fluctuate. If you are using Bitcoin as an investment, it is easy to think that you will always have the same amount of money that you traded in. It is very similar to exchanging your currency to another country's currency. You will either gain or lose value. This is why it is so important to get others to trust the system, too, and use Bitcoin because its value only goes up when its demand goes up!

Please do not forget that you need an online wallet to manage your Bitcoins. Wallets like Coinomi, MyEtherWallet, and Parity all offer you a secure way to keep track of your Bitcoins and store them in a safe place online.

There are also other ways to purchase Bitcoins other than Coinbase. There are states that offer Bitcoins in ATMs across the city. This is made possible through the Bitcoin Depot. If you happen to live in Alabama, <u>Florida, Georgia, Massachusetts, Tennessee, or Texas</u>, this process is easy for you. You will not need to do anything except put money into an ATM and scan the barcode. Within a short amount of time (probably from a few minutes to an hour), you will see Bitcoins in your online wallet, ready for you to spend.

You may want to spend your Bitcoins. The good news is that many places are now accepting Bitcoins, including Cheapair and Dell Computers.

Bitcoin is easier to get through a Bitcoin exchange website if you are buying a substantial amount. This is good if you really want to get involved in the Bitcoin business or want to keep it as an investment. If you live in one of the six lucky states that buy it through an ATM, that is better for smaller transactions.

Overall, there are many ways to buy your Bitcoins. You need to figure out what is best for you. While you are deciding which Bitcoin exchange website to use or what method to use, consider these factors...

- How fast can the Bitcoins get there? It is obviously easier to get a cheaper deal if you can get Bitcoins later and if it is not a current pressing need. When you are pressing for speed, the transfer time for some websites may be longer, and you may not be able to get the cheapest deal.

- What can you use to pay with? If you can pay through a bank account, that makes it so much easier on you because you have to pay less fees. Many websites will charge you a small fee if you want to pay with a credit card.

- How much do you want to buy? Some Bitcoin websites allow you to purchase large amounts, but Coinbase, for example, only lets you buy a thousand Bitcoins at a time (in one day).

You could even become a Bitcoin miner or a "node" yourself! There are different ways that you can do this.

The easiest way but the least efficient way to mine for Bitcoins is to use your own computer's CPU. However, this method is slower and may not help you if you are in the competition to earn Bitcoins. If you are going to go this route, though, you need to make sure that you have an updated graphics card. No, you do not just need that for video games or photo editing. If you want to stay competitive, you need a good graphics card. Newegg.com or

Techbargains might be your best bet to get a cheap but excellent processing card.

There is another way for you to mine, and that is if you get a Field-Programmable Gate Array or FPGA. This is a circuit that you can design just to mine. This is better, but it may not be the best choice either.

CHAPTER 4

HOW DO YOU USE BITCOIN?

Bitcoin can be used for many purposes. You can use it to buy yourself an iPad, bedsheets for your home, or even to pay your workers on the Internet. However, before we jump ahead of ourselves, we should teach you how to send and receive Bitcoins on the Internet.

This is where it gets easier if you have a Coinbase account. Once you have a Coinbase account (as shown in chapter 3), you should open the app and go to your dashboard. Underneath that toolbar, there is a Send and Request button. You can simply enter the name of the recipient and their email address on top of the amount that you want to send to them. You can write a note to them if you so desire, telling them what the Bitcoins are for. From there on, you wait for three confirmations from the miners that are navigating the system, then you can send your transaction, and it goes through to the other person.

Here are some practical uses of Bitcoin in today's world:

- For charitable purposes: You can donate your Bitcoins to the less fortunate.

- You can spend it while doing some online shopping. This is easiest to do through a website that takes Bitcoins. You can go on a website called Overstock. Click here to look for furniture, home decorations, kitchen and outdoor appliances, clothes, jewelry, children's gear and more! https://www.overstock.com/ There are more than a million things that Overstock sells, and this is the perfect place to buy someone a gift or just improve your own home or closet.

- Food. Who does not love food? Many apps allow you to order food with Bitcoins. This is a lot easier if you have an iPhone or an Android phone. There is a famous online website called Bitcoin Restaurants that allows you to order food, even though it may not be available in your state. http://bitcoinrestaurants.net/

- Spend Bitcoin when you go out of home to go somewhere exotic. We have already established that CheapAir has airplane tickets for sale, but there are also other things that you can do while you are away from your home. You can rent a car. You can use Expedia to book airplane tickets as well as hotels, and you can even go on cruises with Ships and Trips Travel.

CHAPTER 5

HOW DO YOU USE BITCOIN IN BUSINESS?

Many small business owners are always excited to expand their business. You may create ads on social media and try to spread the world around everywhere, but few people have looked to Bitcoin!

The truth is that there are many complicated ways to handle business payments, but Bitcoin is not one of them. Bitcoins are easy and simple to deal with. Bitcoin's website lays out their advantages in small businesses, and I am here to show that to you.

In Bitcoin, you do not have to pay a ridiculous amount of fees to transfer money. Even on mainstream websites such as PayPal, it is really hard for people to transfer money without getting charged a ton, especially with large transactions. With Bitcoins, it is cheap and easy for you to transfer large amounts of money to clients.

There is less fraud and deceit with Bitcoin. It has been commonplace to get scammed through websites such as PayPal or any traditional credit card company. You can get charged more than you want and not even notice it. Luckily with Bitcoin's blockchain system, it makes sure that both parties actually have the money, are transferring it over, and that the whole transaction is not sketchy.

You can send Bitcoins fast as opposed to handing cash to someone. Since everything is moving online, why not move money transactions online as well? You can get your money immediately for cheap, even if it is halfway around the world that you are sending it to.

Bitcoin can also be very effective in in your ads, when you accept Bitcoins, you are opening up your business to a whole new market of people who may not have thought about your business at all before. This is a new way to get your name out there.

You can also set it up to where you need multiple people's agreement to send Bitcoins to each other. This prevents one person from trying to take over the business! This helps people negotiate and deal with Bitcoins in a friendly way, and it keeps your business in check. There are many effective ways that customers can pay with Bitcoins.

Here are some ways that you can help incorporate Bitcoins into your business!

- You can pay with Bitcoins in person. Every person with a Bitcoin wallet has a barcode that connects to their account, similar to how Starbucks gift cards have a code as well. This is the easiest way to pay, but it can only be done if you have a Bitcoin wallet. Sign up for one today. For example, this is a good one: https://play.google.com/store/apps/details?id=de.schildbach.wallet

- People can also pay through their Coinbox accounts. This app was actually specifically made for businesses to receive payments. You can enter the amount of the object that you are selling, then it creates a barcode that will receive funds from people. The customer can use a barcode scanner app on either their iPhone or Android phone and scan your code. This allows you to receive their funds.

- Of course, you do not have to go with the two most mainstream methods of paying. You can use a machine called Coinkite. This operates like a credit card machine and allows people to pay in Bitcoins with that method.

In business, there is really not much to Bitcoins except incorporating them as a payment method and maybe buying appliances or supplies for your store with Bitcoins. However, if you do decide to include Bitcoins, you could attract a diverse group of people who are always ready to buy items from you!

Next, we are going to talk about investing in Bitcoin. Keep in mind that it will never be a one hundred percent sure thing because nothing is ever completely foolproof. However, just like stocks, you have the opportunity to excel and make a profit.

CHAPTER 6

HOW DO YOU INVEST IN BITCOIN?

There are many ways that you can use Bitcoins to make a financial return. You have to keep in mind that investing is not always a safe option because the value of things tends to go up and down, but since 2013, the performance of Bitcoins has increased about three hundred percent a year. This cryptocurrency is on the rise.

The best way to invest in Bitcoin would probably be to just go on Coinbase and buy Bitcoins. You can link your bank account through Coinbase, and it also shows you how Bitcoin is doing in the world's marketplace. You can buy Bitcoins through this website very fast, and there is not much of a transition fee.

However, you can also go on a website called BitStamp. You trade Bitcoins with other people that have them, and this allows you to buy and sell Bitcoins whenever you feel like it is on the rise or the fall. Be sure that you pay more attention to the news during this time if you do make this choice because Bitcoin tends to go up when people do not trust the government. Finally, you could go on a Bitcoin exchange or just meet random strangers in public. However, these options are not the safest because they are prone to scam.

Trading Bitcoins

When it comes to trading in the Bitcoin market, the venture has a strong chance of being profitable, regardless if you are coming to cryptocurrency trading with financial market trading experience or if you are brand new to the entire endeavor. The first thing you will need to be aware of is the fact that to trade in cryptocurrency you are going to need to find a cryptocurrency exchange that you are comfortable with. Cryptocurrency exchanges are not regulated or unified in the way that many exchanges are which means you can often find extremely large spreads and lots of fragmentation as well. You will also be able to easily find a margin of at least 20 to 1, if not more. Finally, different exchanges may have different rates, so it is possible to buy low somewhere and sell for a profit somewhere else. Overall, there are plenty of different ways to turn a profit in this space.

Bitcoin has a well-deserved reputation for volatility and is currently considered more than 5 times more volatile than gold and six times as volatile as any of the stocks in the S&P 500. This high degree of volatility tends to create pricing bubbles where upswings are magnified by people looking to get in on the action and downswings are magnified by investors jumping ship to make their money back. Each time a new bubble is formed, it then generates additional hype that will guarantee that Bitcoin makes the news once more. The extra focus provided by the media will then attract additional investors who will then buy in and so on and so forth until the price becomes unsustainable and the bubble bursts. At this point, the hype fades for a type, and the cycle repeats itself.

Compared to other types of investing, the barriers to enter with Bitcoin are few and far between. In general, all you need to do is buy Bitcoins (or portions of Bitcoins), and you are ready to go. If you purchased your Bitcoins before finding your exchange, then you may not even need to verify your account before you are ready to start trading. In addition to other traders, there are also numerous trading companies on the market that offer Bitcoin services through what is known as a contract for differences. These contracts stipulate that the buyer will buy a set number of Bitcoins from the seller and then pay the seller the difference in price between when the contract went into effect and when it expires. If the price decreases during that timeframe, the seller is then required to pay the buyer instead.

It is also possible to find leverage rates as strong as 20 to 1 on contracts for differences. What this means is that if a trader puts down a single Bitcoin on a CF, then they would receive $20 for every $1 increase in price over the specified time frame. While leverage can be useful in some situations, it is very important to be cautious about using it regularly as it can easily work against you instead. As an example, if things had ended up going the other way on the proceeding trade then you would owe $20 for every dollar you invested. Needless to say, this can add up very quickly, especially in trades with hundreds or thousands of shares. As such, it is recommended that new traders stay away from this practice until they are very sure of themselves.

Why Bitcoin trading: First and foremost, Bitcoin is a global currency which means that unlike its more limited contemporaries the price that it is currently worth isn't going to be based on the economy or policies of a specific country. As such, it can react to a wide variety of different stimuli including things like the devaluation of the yuan or the institution of new Capital Controls in Greece. It is also important to keep in mind that many periods of worldwide panic and uncertainty have led to some of Bitcoin's greatest increases. So much so that the issues that Cyprus had with capital control lead to the Bitcoin price bubble of 2013.

No down time: Unlike the other markets, the cryptocurrency market is open 7 days a week, 24 hours a day which means that if you want to buy Bitcoins at 2 AM, then there is absolutely nothing stopping you from pulling the trigger. There are more than 100 cryptocurrency exchanges worldwide, and each is going to determine the price of Bitcoin based on its own personal ledger of trades. What this means is that it is certainly possible to find numbers that are lower in one place than in the other, depending on when you look.

Volatility: As previously discussed, Bitcoin is extremely volatile which means that the potential for profit is extremely high as well. It will regularly swing as much as 5 percent in a single day. Some smaller cryptocurrencies have been known to swing as much as 15 percent in a single day. As a trader, this means you can see significant profits in short order if you manage to get in at the right time, especially if you happen to combine this level of volatility with a significant amount of leverage.

Choosing the right exchange

Choosing the right exchange to trade your Bitcoins in is a very important decision to make, not only because different exchanges are going to vary to a significant degree but because they are not regulated in the way that more traditional exchanges are which means that if they end up taking your money and then closing up shop, there is very little you will be able to do about it. As millions of people have already invested in cryptocurrencies of all sorts, it is clearly a safe process when done properly, it just requires a bit of research on your part up front.

Go local if possible: First and foremost, you are going to want to try to find an exchange that is based in your home country. This way there is more of a chance that, if the exchange does have some oversight, you will actually see your money again should things go poorly. This is still not a guarantee, but it is better than nothing. Using a local exchange will also make it easier to get in touch with a live person should you need assistance as you will be in the same time zone. Finally, considering the time zone of your exchange is also important as matching time zones will make it easier for you to trade at points when the trade volume is highest.

When choosing a local exchange, it is important to double check that they trade in the currency that you are planning to use as not all exchanges trade in their country's national currency. Make sure to read the fine print on the exchange you are considering and get a look at their options to avoid having to pay extra transaction fees before you can even get started.

Be aware of purchasing practices: As Bitcoin exchanges aren't tied to any official exchange, there is no guarantee in place when it comes to how it will handle the process of purchasing Bitcoins. Depending on where they are located they may take PayPal, wire transfers, credit cards or direct bank deposits. You are going to need to ensure that the exchange is reliable before providing them with this level of information and you may want to initially purchase your Bitcoins elsewhere and then transfer them in to your trading account. This way you can know what you are really in for and ensure you are not just padding a scammer's pockets before you use the exchange directly.

The first thing you are going to want to do is to read the reviews from other users of the exchange to ensure that they are largely positive. While a few bad reviews are nothing to be worried about, if the reviews you see all have a specific complaint in common, then this should be considered a red flag, and you will likely want to look elsewhere. Additionally, you are going to want to ensure that they are using an HTTPS URL as this means that there are additional security protocols in place. Finally, you will want to ensure that you have to enter a password, plus a dual factor authentication in order to log into the exchange to guarantee that your funds are as safe as possible.

Check into exchange fees: When you buy Bitcoins, the transaction fee that comes with the purchase partially goes to Bitcoin to fund the blockchain and partially to the miner or miners who verified the transaction. While transaction fees are typically technically voluntary, declining to pay them often means that your block will take much longer to be verified. The cost to verify a Bitcoin transaction is about $3. In addition to this fee, you will also need to pay an exchange a fee to use their system. Even with the extra cost, the fees for trading in cryptocurrency are typically lower than those of other markets.

Nevertheless, it is important to give this facet of the exchange a consideration before you get started as the fees exchanges charge can vary dramatically. You are going to want to consider the current going rate and then choose an exchange that is right in line with it. Going above is obviously going to cut into your bottom line so and should be avoided, but going below should also be avoided because it shows the exchange is desperate for customers and could potentially be a scam.

Look at the order book: If an exchange has a volume level to be proud of, then they are going to happily publish their order book for everyone to see. Generally, it is going to be a good idea to avoid going through an exchange that is unwilling to show off their decentralized ledger. The reason behind this reluctance could be that they are what is known as a *fractional exchange* which means they are unable to pay out all of their debts at once.

Transparency: Outside of the order book, it is important that your exchange of choice is as transparent as possible on a few other topics as well. Taken together, the following means that they have nothing to hide when it comes to their particular business model and are thus likely to be a reliable place to keep your investments.

If an exchange is truly working at maximum transparency, then they will be willing to provide their cold storage address as well as any details relating to the verification of their reserves. Additionally, you will want to keep an eye out for Bitcoin audits as they are another way that exchanges reach out to their customer and provide proof that they have enough to cover their required liquidity, right here, right now.

ETA: Bitcoin transactions require verification which means that you are not going to be able to receive your Bitcoins instantaneously, this means it is important to find an exchange that imposes a hold on your Bitcoins for the shortest period of time possible. Likewise, you are going to want to ensure that your chosen exchange locks in your rate at the time of purchase, not the time of verification as doing the reverse means a good trade could easily turn sour before your verification goes through.

Anonymity is key: The Bitcoin philosophy is built around anonymity, do not let your exchange take that away from you. To keep your transactions as under the radar as possible you are going to want to ensure that you purchase your Bitcoins before joining the exchange and then adding your coins directly. Take precautions and ensure that your exchange allows for no verification with this payment method, otherwise you will have committed to a more connected choice.

CHAPTER 7

HOW SECURE IS BITCOIN?

Bitcoin is mainly secure through the Blockchain system. To learn more about Blockchain, please refer to Chapter 2. With the Blockchain system, there are many things that you can ensure does not happen with your Bitcoins.

1) You can make sure that there is no one double spending your Bitcoins. Every block in the encryption ledger secures many transactions with special codes. If a code is repeated, miners look back to check and see if they are the same Bitcoins trying to be spent on two different things. Because people do not want Bitcoins to be missing and there are only twenty-one million of them, the miners often report this activity and deny the transaction if they see that Bitcoins are being spent two times.

2) Bitcoin has a system called the SHA 256 encryption system. This security code verifies your transactions and ensures that your money does not go where it should not go.

3) There is a thing called two-factor authentication that ensures that you are the one sending your Bitcoins. By inputting a phone number that allows you to get a code on your cell phone and enter it into your payment website, this ensures that you are the person who is sending your Bitcoins unless your cell phone is also stolen. Two-factor authentication has protected emails for ages, but it also protects Bitcoins and your money.

Avoiding fraud with Bitcoin

Because Bitcoin is extremely unregulated, it is natural for schemers and fraudsters to always be on the lookout for the next big thing when it comes to duping people out of their money. It is important that you be aware of the scams that are outlined below, but also remember that new types are bound to appear as time goes on. In general, you are going to want to always be on your guard to ensure that you keep your money safe.

False Bitcoin exchanges: While some Bitcoin exchanges are less well liked then others, most at least have the intention of providing reliable service to their customers. False Bitcoin exchanges have no such intentions and are going to be nothing but a way to take your money and run. The most reliable way to spot a false exchange is via their advertisements. If a site is promising a flat rate for Bitcoins, and especially if they are offering a rate that is below the current level of the market then there is going to be an extremely good chance that they are running a scam. A Bitcoin exchange functions just like any other exchange which means that it has buyers and sellers. No seller is going to sell for below market value, that is why it is the market value. In Bitcoin exchanges, as in life, if something appears too good to be true, it probably is.

Another key red flag to be on the lookout for is if the exchange is offering to buy your Bitcoins through PayPal directly. Remember, this is not the way that exchanges work. If you sign up for an exchange, then your Bitcoins do not leave your account until after they have sold. In general, this type of scam will require you to present your PayPal information and then provide you will find a QR code where you can send your Bitcoins. After your Bitcoins are gone, the promised payment will never materialize. For your own protection, it is best to never enter into any transactions that aren't through an official exchange.

Phony Bitcoin wallets: It can be more difficult to spot a fake wallet than a fake exchange because many scam wallets may actually appear to work as intended, stealing your information the whole while. You are going to want to keep an eye out for malware with these types of scams which means you are going to start by downloading the wallet from Bitcoin.com instead.

If you do want to use a third-party wallet, then you will need to start by putting faith in your instincts and checking to ensure the website is using an HTTPS secure Internet protocol. You will also want to check the URL to make sure that it is the URL of a trusted Bitcoin wallet and not a close approximation of the same. If it looks like the goal of the site is to make it appear to be legitimate, but it is actually a knockoff then there is a safe bet that it is a scam. If the wallet comes with a downloadable client, then you are going to want to test the executable for any malware before installation.

You are also going to want to verify the quality of any wallet through the Bitcoin subreddit community to ensure that your cryptocurrency is going to be safe in its new home.

Phishing scams: Another type of scam that you will see on the regular is the phishing scam. In this scenario, the scammer will attempt to trick you into thinking they are an official either from an exchange you use or possibly from Bitcoin itself. This type of approach will typically come through email, though false advertisements are also an option. The best way to defeat this type of scam is to keep an eye out for clues such as the URL that the email urges you to click on or the email address of the person who sent it. As a rule of thumb, you will want to avoid links in unknown emails, as well as attachments. If you do feel the need to contact the company in question then always do so through official channels. Send a separate email or call their customer service and explain your situation. This will ensure your personal information remains safe.

CHAPTER 8

HOW DO YOU REMAIN ANONYMOUS WITH BITCOIN?

Bitcoin is supposed to be an anonymous currency that protects your identity wherever you go. Unfortunately, just like anything else on the Internet, it is not completely anonymous.

There are natural things that Bitcoin does to keep you somewhat anonymous. For one, you can hide behind your online wallet. Bitcoin does not tell people your actual name. In fact, it presents you as a string of letters and numbers that are randomly generated. This means that people do not have to know who you are, your name, or your location and address.

However, Bitcoin is not completely anonymous. After all, with Blockchain, it is a currency located on a public financial ledger. Every transaction you make is online, whether you like it or not. You cannot simply hide that because it is what makes Bitcoin fundamentally accountable and safe. However, there are many steps that you can take to ensure that your financial activity and personal information stay safe, even in the ridiculously insane world that is Bitcoin.

First of all, there are many methods that you can take that are not technical at all. The first one of all is a no brainer. It is to never share your wallet code with anyone that you know. It does not matter if it is a close friend, best friend, or even a family member. Once someone knows your wallet code, he or she can know about every transaction you make through the public blockchain. Not only should you not tell them your code, but you also should not post anything about what you spend on social media. This includes Instagram, Facebook, Twitter, and any other online accounts you have. There are few ways to protect your information once someone gets a hold of your it and decides to use it against you.

Another way is to change your wallet information every time that you use it. You can have a "throwaway address" every time that you use a wallet. Every time that you make a transaction, you can change your wallet address to a new one. This is called a "Bitcoin Core" client. This will help you change your address whenever you decide to spend your Bitcoins. You do not have to spend over any specific amount; it will change your address anyway. These new addresses can be linked whenever you spend money though because the Blockchain can put together all the transactions spent at the same company. In some cases, if you really want to keep your identity a secret, it is easier for you to just go ahead and create a new wallet account. There are also specific sellers that you should avoid. Avoid "hosted clients" who make you give out your keys to any third-party servers. All of your entry codes are generated on third party servers with this type of company, making it really easy for your information to be stolen.

There are also other ways that involve more technical apps to ensure your safety. These apps will protect you from having your IP Address tracked, which is your physical Internet address.

One of these methods is through an app called TOR. This is a website that hides your IP address. Once you install the program, you can go to the website of wherever you get your Bitcoins. Connect it to a proxy, and you can use your Bitcoins for transactions, and no one would even know.

Another way you can hide your IP address is through a very traditional way called VPN. This is like a proxy server, but it is much easier to use. You only have to turn it on whenever you make a transaction. You can install this on your cell phone or your computer. Popular VPNs are all around, and VPNExpress is a very good choice.

If you are not good with all this technical stuff, another option for you is to use a public network, such as the Wifi at McDonald's or the mall closest to you. When you use public Wifi, Internet providers do not know your information. You do not have to say where you live or even give your name to be using a public Wifi or a public computer. However, using a public Wifi is also risky because it may save your passwords on the computer. Be sure you are logged out when you use this sort of network.

You can also buy Bitcoins anonymously, but every time you use a Bitcoin exchange website, you have to provide your own personal information. It is easier for you to avoid websites like these altogether, because they ask for your personal information. To keep it safe, you might want to just buy Bitcoins from people near you and exchange it in person for cash. You can use a website called Local Bitcoins to find people who are willing to do this. When you do this, be sure you stay safe as well, and see if the seller has any feedback or history records from other people who have bought from them. You do not want to meet in a shady place where they could scam you, so keep it public. Try Local Bitcoins.

You can also buy Bitcoins in the mail. This keeps things anonymous, but you may also get scammed if you mail cash to get Bitcoins. However, you can take pictures of the package to prove that you have sent it out if legal matters ever come up.

You can also buy Bitcoins from an ATM and keep it anonymous. Some machines do not require you to put our personal information in; rather, they just give you Bitcoins if you give them cash. This might be the best option if you want to keep it anonymous, but can be difficult to find.

You can also safely get Bitcoins by working online jobs. Beware, though, because some online jobs are not actually legit and will scam you. You can look for jobs on Reddit, Pinterest, Instagram, and Twitter. Many of them involve data entries or writing for a company. Other online jobs will allow you to earn money by watching advertisements, but those do not pay enough for you to consider them as substantial work. Finally, you can mine for Bitcoins. You can hope to earn the Bitcoins by being the first to crack the code, but this, unfortunately, does not always happen.

You can only hope to earn money from this if you have a really fast, powerful processor. Those Bitcoin miners are also not often sold, and many people get scammed while buying that too. This does keep it completely anonymous, but it is hard to come by and generally not worth your effort.

Finally, there are also methods that allow you to collaborate with others and stay anonymous. One way you can do this is through the CoinJoin method. By using this method, you can pool together different people who want to spend money. No one will be able to tell who spent what just because everyone is pulled together into one transaction.

Finally, there is an option called DarkWallet. This is still a new project, and it is not completely finished yet. There are betas released, but this basically creates a safe wallet that keeps you anonymous. You have CoinJoin projects with other people. There, you will have secret wallet addresses that cannot go public. The best thing about this is that you can access it directly on your Internet browser, whether that be Internet Explorer, Google Chrome, or Firefox.

CHAPTER 9

WHY IS BITCOIN SO POPULAR?

Yeah, Bitcoin is good, and it gets better. But why is it so popular right now? Why is it in such high demand? The truth is that there are both pros and cons to Bitcoin, but the pros heavily outweigh the cons. Here are more reasons why Bitcoin is loved by so many people:

1) Bitcoin is very fast. Bitcoin is the one currency that you can send, and it will arrive at the other person's account just a few seconds or minutes later! At a bank, you often have to wait so many days before you can access the coins. That is not true with Bitcoin! Bitcoins allow you to be able to transfer money to someone's account even if they are halfway across the world and you do not have to pay transaction fees on top of that.

2) Bitcoin barely has any transaction fees. Normally, sending money to a whole bunch of people internationally would take so much money. It might even equal the amount of

money that you are sending over to them. With Bitcoin, this is not a problem, as it often takes just as much to send one penny as it does to send a million dollars to the other person. Even though credit cards are just as fast, credit cards are so much more expensive that you do not even want to think about getting near one half the time. In some cases, it may even be free to send a Bitcoin to a friend. You never really know until you take the chance to explore the currency in a way that you have not before.

3) Bitcoin is easy to use. You can simply sign up for an account online and never have to worry about confusing questions. Bank accounts take forever to set up, but Bitcoin accounts require an email address, and that is basically it.

4) Bitcoins do not inflate with the government currency. In the United States, if we do not have enough money to pay off our spending costs, the Federal Reserve Board will keep printing money and devalue everything that we have. Our money is so affected by the economy when we choose to put all of our investments in one country. This is particularly bad if you do not have a country with stable politics. When you use Bitcoin, only twenty-one million coins are floating around, and there are no more that can be printed until 2040. That means that there is no inflation currently, as long as you trust in the system and everyone else does too. This makes Bitcoin the best!

5) You can remain anonymous with Bitcoin. It is a person, and you do not have to link your name, address, or phone

number, or email to any of the websites. You can have more than one Bitcoin account if you like, and no one is stopping you. No one has to know how much money you have, unlike if you gave them a wallet and let them borrow a few dollars. Bitcoin is yours and yours alone to manage.

6) It is transparent and safe. Some blockchains allow people to keep each other in check. You do not have to worry about people ripping you off and not having any money. For your sake, everyone will be honest about each other's transactions.

7) Many countries are using Bitcoins now. It appears to be the currency of the future, and everything is rapidly moving online. Not only is America using it, but Australia and the United Kingdom are also taking up the offer of Bitcoin lately. Some websites allow you to get Bitcoins in all of these countries now, and many people believe in it.

8) Once Bitcoins have been sent, they are completely gone. There is no way for the sender to regret what they did and take it back. This keeps all orders honest as well.

9) You do not have to erase government currency completely, but you can add an extra source of income with Bitcoin. Even though mining may not be very productive most of the time, it is still an extra source of income that you can get without much effort! You could probably earn cash while you are asleep.

10) There is no government involved. There is no one central person controlling everyone's money affairs unlike all the currencies of the world. That means that one government's mistake cannot affect everyone who has Bitcoins.

11) It is harder for people to steal Bitcoins from you since you have both a public and a private key that you keep to yourself. Blockchain servers and miners are ensuring that people do not spend what they do not have. This protects you as both a seller and a consumer.

12) You do not have to deal with programs such as PayPal. You do not have to deal with people freezing your money or not giving it to you until a certain date. You do not have to deal with people removing random money out of your account. Bitcoin is yours to control 100%.

13) There is much political tension going on right now, and traditional money could have very volatile values that you do not want to trust. Tensions are great between America, China, Russia, North Korea, and various other countries. If you trust in the government, it is easy for your money to render useless.

14) You do not need to trust any banks to manage your money for you.

Because there are so many pros to the Bitcoin system, many people overlook the fact that it is a new, quasi-established and untested to stand up to political forces as of yet.

On the other hand, there is a reason why we do not use government money as much when there are newer inventions. This is because the government really aims to control, and you will learn why in the next chapter.

CHAPTER 10

WHAT ARE THE CONSEQUENCES OF GOVERNMENT MONEY?

These are the common problems when using traditional fiat money, such as:

1) **Inflation**

   Government money is prone to inflation when times are bad, and the economy is falling. It is not easy for the government to simply pick up their feet and come back up, but rather they over-compensate by printing out a lot more money. This causes all your cash to devalue rather than keep up with everyone else's money. You do not want to fall victim to inflation, so you really do not want to use government money all the time.

2) **Control and No Privacy**

   The government keeps the charge of whatever transactions you make, and it is hard for you to keep it private if you do not want everyone else knowing about what you spend it on or how much you spent. This helps keep your money anonymous and safe.

3) **You do not have to go through the banks if you do not use government money**

Banks often charge insane amounts of interest that tend to make people lose money rather than earn it. Without using government money, you can bypass all of this and keep it safe.

CHAPTER 11

HOW TO START USING BITCOIN: (LINKS INCLUDED)

Simple steps anyone can do now:

Step 1: Purchase Bitcoins. You can buy your Bitcoins off of any Bitcoin exchange website, and here are a couple of sites that you can go to that are trustworthy.

https://www.bitcoin.com/buy-bitcoin

https://www.coinbase.com/buy-bitcoin?locale=en-US

Once you have your Bitcoins, you must create a wallet to store all of it in there. *(Coinbase now has wallets)*

https://bitcoin.org/en/choose-your-wallet

Go to this link so you can pick a wallet that suits you, and be sure you keep it safe and do not give out your personal code.

Step 2: Get started using Bitcoin now by using it to pay for things. You can use Bitcoin to pay for various things securely through a website known as BitPay. This website allows you to transfer Bitcoins to places that take it.

https://bitpay.com/

After following these steps, you can now use Bitcoin on whatever you desire. You can use it for mining, if you want, or you can use it for investing, or you can simply just spend it. The choice is up to you..

CONCLUSION

The world is changing rapidly, but you cannot deny that Bitcoin is a possible currency of the future.

Bitcoin and cryptocurrency are growing very fast, but it's not yet quite a sure thing. Governments have not done anything significant yet to stop or impede cryptocurrency, except for China. We do not know how much it threatens their centralized banking structure. **Keep this fact in mind while investing or buying bitcoins or any cryptocurrency, have a contingency plan in place in case there is a capitulation event.**

As always, we would really appreciate a review on Amazon Kindle! Please let us know your thoughts so that we can improve in the future.

www.ingramcontent.com/pod-product-compliance
Lightning Source LLC
Chambersburg PA
CBHW050243230526
45470CB00005B/2087